I0519587

THE LEGACY PLAYBOOK

PLAYS TO SECURE YOUR FAMILY'S FUTURE

FRAN L. RAYNOR

If you purchased this book without a cover, you should be aware that this book is stolen property. It was reported as "unsold and destroyed" to the publisher, and neither the author nor the publisher has received any payment for this "stripped book."

ISBN: 978-1-957443-13-3

The Legacy Playbook

Copyright © 2024 by Francina Raynor. Printed in the United States of America.

All rights reserved. This book or parts thereof may not be reproduced in any form, stored in any retrieval system, or transmitted in any form by any means — electronic, mechanical, photocopy, recording, or otherwise — without prior written permission of the author, except as provided by United States of America copyright law.

For permission requests, please contact the author via email at fra9058984@gmail.com.

Cover courtesy of T'Mia Raynor
Photographs courtesy of Philip Raynor, PRR Photography

First printing edition 2024

JayMedia Publishing
Laurel, MD 20708
www.publishing.jaymediagroup.net

This Playbook Belongs To:

DISCLAIMER

This workbook should be kept confidential, in a safe place so that it cannot be accessed by anyone that would abuse it.
Make sure to share this information with your designated emergency contact or store it securely in a bank safety deposit box.
If they are unaware of your arrangements, accessing information or funds may prove difficult.

LEGAL NOTICE

This workbook has been prepared for informational purposes only and is not intended to serve as legal advice. The content contained herein is not created by a lawyer, and its use should not be construed as establishing an attorney-client relationship.

While efforts have been made to ensure the accuracy, completeness, and timeliness of the information provided, no guarantee is made regarding its suitability or applicability to individual circumstances. Readers are advised to seek professional legal advice from a qualified attorney regarding their specific estate planning needs, particularly concerning end-of-life matters. Each individual's situation may vary, and legal requirements can change over time and across jurisdictions.

By utilizing this workbook, you acknowledge and agree that the creators and distributors of this material shall not be held liable for any damages or losses arising from its use or reliance upon its contents.

Your use of this workbook constitutes your acceptance of these terms and understanding that it is not a substitute for personalized legal counsel.

DEDICATION

This is dedicated to those who shaped me into who I am today: my parents, Marea and Norris Roy; foster mother, Mary Brown; brother, Norris W. Roy; Aunt and Uncle Dorothy and Sherman Tynes; and Uncle William Ford. They each contributed to my growth with nurtured love, faith, hope, and support. My motivation for undertaking this project stems from my deep desire to leave a lasting legacy for my family. This book would not be possible without God. I am a firm believer that He allows us to walk in our passion. I truly believe this is the path in which He is directing me and for that I am extremely grateful.

ACKNOWLEDGMENTS

I would like to first thank my sons, Philip and Sean, for their unconditional love is a constant blessing in my life. My brother Kenny's support during this book publishing process has been invaluable. I give a special thank you to T'Mia, my daughter-in-love, for wholeheartedly taking on this project, designing the workbook, and helping fulfill a dream I've pursued for two years. I cherish my four grandchildren Kennedy, Peyton, Jeremiah, and Portland, each with their unique personalities. Ensuring their well-being and providing for their future has been my driving force in this endeavor. I'm grateful to Jaelin, my niece, for her swift support in bringing the project to completion.

I would like to express my sincere appreciation to the Roy, Drake, Weatherspoon, Rogers, Perry, and McDaniel families for their constant love and support throughout this process; and to Gwendolyn Baccus & Mable Rogers, my mentors and mother figures, who consistently lift me in prayer and hold me up through it all. A special acknowledgment goes to Christine Johnson and JayMedia Publishing for stepping in at the last minute ensuring the professional quality of the product.

Lastly, thank you to Pastor Perrin for his constant support and encouragement, and for seeing something in me that I didn't even see in myself in achieving this goal. To each and every individual mentioned, and to those unintentionally left unnamed, your invaluable contributions have played a significant role in the success of this workbook.

PREFACE

I'm so proud of you and how you have always looked out for others…such selfless love!! You have been the bedrock for our family as we have experienced end-of-life heartaches with the passing of our Dad, Mom, Brother, Aunt, Uncle, and many, many friends and relatives.

These are very difficult and traumatic times and it takes a selfless person like yourself to put aside their hurts and to focus on others to "get the job done" of meeting people in the midst of their heartaches and allowing them the time to grieve as you prepared for their loved one's journey to meet Jesus.

Unfortunately, in our communities, we don't do an adequate job of preparing for these end-of-life events, and families are left trying to figure out how to distribute any assets our loved ones may have had regardless of how big or small they may be.

This workbook allows everyone to prepare for the day that will come for all of us … no exceptions! Death is at each one of our doors so having an estate plan with assets in line with our wishes is invaluable. Thank you so much for embarking on this journey to help all of us!!

Take pleasure in the following 2 verses as they represent the essence of you!

Philippians 2:3 - *"Do nothing out of selfish ambition or vain conceit. Rather, in humility [and love] value others above yourselves"*
Luke 6:23 - *"Rejoice in that day [when you meet Jesus] and leap for joy because great is your reward in Heaven."*

Love You Sis and I don't know what I would do without you!!

- **Kenny,** *brother*

Resourceful, comprehensive, and helpful are just a few words that come to mind when I think of Fran. Indeed, in the pages of this book, you will see these qualities, in particular, shine forth brightly. From tons of hands-on experience, knowledge building, expertise, and drawing on her wealth of relational capital, Fran has meticulously and yet compassionately curated what you hold in your hands. This game plan is thorough and, at the same time, approachable as it covers every facet needed to make sure our legacy outlives us. We thank you, Fran, for your labor of love, care, and concern to ensure we're thinking beyond ourselves and helping us understand the importance of these critical life legacy matters.

- Pastor Perrin Rogers

I'm elated and extremely excited to celebrate my dear friend, Fran. She's embarking on and pursuing her life goals. Ever since I have known her, she has had a way of selfless serving and ministering to others, which carries a special greatness. It can be overlooked or taken for granted by so many, but never overlooked by God. Fran is deliberate in walking in her God-given passion and uniqueness, using her gifts, talents, and abilities to fulfill her life purpose.

Fran, thank God for you and one day you will hear Him say "Well done, good and faithful servant" (Matt. 25:21).

I'm keenly aware that Fran has personally seen families suffer due to a lack of legacy and end-of-life planning. Therefore, she has pursued this project of educating, informing, and helping families plan and better prepare for the inevitable. She strongly believes and has invested so much that no one at the time of sorrow and loss should experience regret and lack of preparation for his/her loved ones and family. None of us like to think about what happens to our family if we pass, but Fran offers us a smart way to free them from a burden... and give them peace of mind.

The wealth of information that Fran has presented is invaluable. Please listen, pay attention, and be smart. You will have no regrets!

- Mable Rogers, *best friend*

TABLE OF CONTENTS

☐ Introduction 1

☐ **Play 1: Background**

☐ Personal 3
☐ Family and Dependent Information 5
☐ Instructions for Care of Dependents. 7
☐ Pets 8
☐ Affiliations 9
☐ Close Friends and Family 10

☐ **Play 2: Contact**

☐ Emergency Contacts. 14
☐ Legal Contacts. 15
☐ Business Contacts 16

☐ **Play 3: Medical**

☐ Healthcare Information. 20
☐ Medical History 22
☐ Medications 23
☐ In Case of Incapacitation 25

☐ **Play 4: Finances**

☐ Bills. 28
☐ Debts. 29
☐ Credit and Debit Cards 30
☐ Bank accounts 32
☐ Investments 34
☐ Retirement 36
☐ Safes and Safe Deposit Boxes 37
☐ Hidden Cash 38
☐ Finance Apps 39
☐ Additional Assets 40

☐ **Play 5: Security**

☐ Passwords 43
☐ Security Questions. 44
☐ Codes 45
☐ Location of Important Documents. 46
☐ Description and Location of Keys 48

☐ **Play 6: The Final Play**

☐ Final Affairs 51
☐ Final Expenses. 53

INTRODUCTION

When I was growing up, discussions about illness or the passing of a family member were never part of our conversations. It wasn't until I got older that I realized how important it is to have one's affairs organized. Through life's experiences, I've witnessed the challenges faced by families when crucial information isn't documented. My goal is to equip you with the tools needed to proactively make these decisions so the burden doesn't fall on your loved ones in the future. I believe it is important, even starting at the age of 18, to have a roadmap in place for unforeseen emergencies, ensuring trusted loved ones have access to vital financial, medical, and security information.

I understand you may be wondering, "Where do I even start?" Getting your affairs in order is simpler than you might think, and it begins with this playbook. I've laid out a play-by-play guide to help walk you through this process to not only prepare for the end of life but also to live fully in the present, crafting a legacy that reflects your desires.

We have to change our way of thinking and address these processes before they become urgent. Instead of dwelling on the uncertainty of when we'll leave this earth—a matter known only to God—let's focus on practical preparations. For example, consider how common it is for families to face confusion when someone falls ill, with bills to pay and/or conflicting opinions on the best course of action moving forward. The solution lies in proactive planning: documenting your wishes and appointing a trusted loved one to lead decision-making.

This is how I ensure clarity and unity for myself and my family during challenging times, and I aim for you to achieve the same for yourself and your loved ones.

- **Fran**

"By wisdom a house is built, and by understanding it is established."
Proverbs 24:3 (ESV)

Play 1: Background

Welcome to the first play in your legacy playbook! This play will guide you through gathering important personal information. It will help your loved ones handle things smoothly if you ever face tough situations like serious illness, injury, hospitalization, incapacity, or passing away.

- **PERSONAL**
  - Employment
  - Military
  - Education
  - Additional Personal Information
- **FAMILY AND DEPENDENT INFORMATION**
  - Spouse/Partner
  - Parents
  - Sibling(s)
  - Grandchildren
  - Dependent(s)
- **INSTRUCTIONS FOR CARE OF DEPENDENTS**
- **PETS**
- **AFFILIATIONS**
  - Religious/Places of Worship
  - Greek Fraternities/Sororities
  - Other Associations
- **CLOSE FRIENDS AND FAMILY**

TESTIMONIAL

The term "getting your affairs in order" can often have a negative connotation since many people relate it to end-of-life events, which can be scary. However, getting things in order and organizing assets/information for your family can make things so much easier for the future as well as the present. This was something that Fran helped me and my family to see as she would always suggest that we start planning for the future. Knowing where to even begin was overwhelming, but working with Fran helped to make the process less stressful. The help and resources she provided were immeasurable and seeing this workbook come together, I know it will help many.

- T'Mia Raynor

PERSONAL

Full Legal Name: _____

Maiden Name: _____ Other Names: _____

Phone: _____

Email: _____

Home Address: _____

Mailing Address: _____

State ID / Driver's License Number: _____

Date of Birth: _____ Birthplace: _____

Location of Birth Certificate/Citizenship Papers: _____

State/Country: _____

Social Security (SS) Number: _____

Location of SS Card: _____

Employment

Name of Employer #1: _____

Job Title: _____

Date of Employment: _____

Employer Address: _____

Website: _____ Phone: _____

Contact Person: _____

Name of Employer #2: _____

Job Title: _____

Date of Employment: _____

Employer Address: _____

Website: _____ Phone: _____

Contact Person: _____

Military

Military Branch: _____

Rank/Pay Grade: _____

Service Dates: _____

Status: _____

Discharge Date: _____

Veterans Affairs Phone: _____

Military Benefit/Insurance Detail: _____

Location of Military Records: _____

Education

School Attended/State/Year(s): _____

School Attended/State/Year(s): _____

School Attended/State/Year(s): _____

School Attended/State/Year(s): _____

School Attended/State/Year(s): _____

Additional Personal Information

_____

_____

_____

_____

_____

_____

_____

_____

_____

_____

_____

_____

_____

FAMILY AND DEPENDENT INFORMATION

Spouse/Partner

Full Legal Name: _____

Date of Birth: _____ Social Security Number: _____

Address: _____

Phone: _____

Email: _____

Former Spouse Full Legal Name: _____

Date of Birth: _____ Social Security Number: _____

Contact Information *(Phone, Email, Address)*: _____

_____

Parents

Mother's Name/Maiden Name: _____

Date of Birth: _____ Social Security Number: _____

Contact Information *(Phone, Email, Address)*: _____

_____

Father's Name: _____

Date of Birth: _____ Social Security Number: _____

Contact Information *(Phone, Email, Address)*: _____

_____

Sibling(s)

#1 Full Legal Name: _____

Date of Birth: _____ Social Security Number: _____

Contact Information *(Phone, Email, Address)*: _____

_____

#2 Full Legal Name: _____

Date of Birth: _____ Social Security Number: _____

Contact Information *(Phone, Email, Address)*: _____

_____

#3 Full Legal Name: _____

Date of Birth: _____ Social Security Number: _____

Contact Information *(Phone, Email, Address)*: _____

_____

Dependent(s)

#1 Full Legal Name: _____

Date of Birth: _____ Social Security Number: _____

Contact Information *(Phone, Email, Address)*: _____

_____

#2 Full Legal Name: _____

Date of Birth: _____ Social Security Number: _____

Contact Information *(Phone, Email, Address)*: _____

_____

#3 Full Legal Name: _____

Date of Birth: _____ Social Security Number: _____

Contact Information *(Phone, Email, Address)*: _____

_____

#4 Full Legal Name: _____

Date of Birth: _____ Social Security Number: _____

Contact Information *(Phone, Email, Address)*: _____

_____

INSTRUCTIONS FOR CARE OF DEPENDENTS

Dependent #1 Name: _____

Primary Care Physician: _____

Contact: _____

Health Conditions: _____

Documentation Location: _____

Guardian to be Named: _____ Contact: _____

Instructions for Care: _____

_____

_____

Dependent #2 Name: _____

Primary Care Physician: _____

Contact: _____

Health Conditions: _____

Documentation Location: _____

Guardian to be Named: _____ Contact: _____

Instructions for Care: _____

_____

_____

Dependent #3 Name: _____

Primary Care Physician: _____

Contact: _____

Health Conditions: _____

Documentation Location: _____

Guardian to be Named: _____ Contact: _____

Instructions for Care: _____

_____

_____

PETS

Name: _____

Description *(ex. type, breed, etc.)*: _____

Date of Birth: _____

Health Conditions: _____

Medications: _____

Veterinarian: _____

Address: _____

Phone and Email: _____

Guardian/Person to care for a pet: _____

Contact Information *(address, phone, email)*: _____

Location of Documents *(ex. registration, medical, care instructions)*: _____

Notes *(ex. food, feeding instructions, habits, etc.)*: _____

_____

_____

#2 Name: _____

Description *(ex. type, breed, etc.)*: _____

Date of Birth: _____

Health Conditions: _____

Medications: _____

Veterinarian: _____

Address: _____

Phone and Email: _____

Guardian/Person to care for a pet: _____

Contact Information *(address, phone, email)*: _____

Location of Documents *(ex. registration, medical, care instructions)*: _____

Notes *(ex. food, feeding instructions, habits, etc.)*: _____

_____

_____

AFFILIATIONS

Religious/Place(s) of Worship

Name: _____

Address: _____

Phone: _____

Website: _____

Contact Person: _____

Name: _____

Address: _____

Phone: _____

Website: _____

Contact Person: _____

Greek Sororities/Fraternities

Name: _____

Address: _____

Phone: _____

Website: _____

Contact Person: _____

Name: _____

Address: _____

Phone: _____

Website: _____

Contact Person: _____

Other Associations

Name: _____

Address: _____

Phone: _____

Website: _____

Contact Person: _____

Name: _____

Address: _____

Phone: _____

Website: _____

Contact Person: _____

CLOSE FRIENDS & FAMILY

Name: _____

Relationship: _____

Address: _____

Phone: _____

Email: _____

Name: _____

Relationship: _____

Address: _____

Phone: _____

Email: _____

Name: _____

Relationship: _____

Address: _____

Phone: _____

Email: _____

Name: _____

Address: _____

Phone: _____

Website: _____

Contact Person: _____

Name: _____

Address: _____

Phone: _____

Website: _____

Contact Person: _____

Name: _____

Address: _____

Phone: _____

Website: _____

Contact Person: _____

Name: _____

Address: _____

Phone: _____

Website: _____

Contact Person: _____

Name: _____

Address: _____

Phone: _____

Website: _____

Contact Person: _____

"Not everything that is faced can be changed, but nothing can be changed until it is faced."   *– James Baldwin*

Play 1 Notes:

_____
_____
_____
_____
_____
_____
_____
_____
_____
_____
_____
_____
_____
_____
_____
_____
_____
_____
_____
_____
_____
_____
_____
_____

Play 2: Contacts

In this next play, we'll focus on gathering details about who you'd want to reach out to in case of personal, legal, or business emergencies.

- **EMERGENCY CONTACTS**
- **LEGAL CONTACTS**
  - Attorney
  - Power of Attorney
  - Estate Executor
  - Tax Preparer
  - Trustee
  - Title
- **BUSINESS CONTACTS**
  - Main Business Information
  - Associates, Employees & Contractors

TESTMONIAL

All I can say is…. Fran is HEAVEN SENT! It's literally how I feel when I see her walk in her passion. Not only have I watched her but I have experienced her work and passion first hand. I had an elderly couple who were neighbors of mine that I kinda took in to watch and keep my eyes on them since their children lived on the other side of the country. Unfortunately, the wife passed away. The husband relied heavily on his wife. He needed assistance making arrangements and taking care of everything related to his wife's services. I did not know how to support him, but I quickly referred him to someone I knew who could connect him with all of the resources he would need. Fran was able to help him make all of the arrangements and ensure that everything was taken handled. She doesn't just stop there. She makes sure that you are satisfied and you are not in need of anything else. Long story short Fran is passionate about her work and the person as a whole. HEAVEN SENT!!!

- Tiffany Weatherspoon

EMERGENCY CONTACTS

Primary Name: _____

Relationship/Title: _____ *Are they aware of this planner? (Y/N)*

Address: _____

Phone: _____ Email: _____

Notes: _____

Secondary Name: _____

Relationship/Title: _____ *Are they aware of this planner? (Y/N)*

Address: _____

Phone: _____ Email: _____

Notes: _____

Secondary Name: _____

Relationship/Title: _____ *Are they aware of this planner? (Y/N)*

Address: _____

Phone: _____ Email: _____

Notes: _____

Secondary Name: _____

Relationship/Title: _____ *Are they aware of this planner? (Y/N)*

Address: _____

Phone: _____ Email: _____

Notes: _____

Secondary Name: _____

Relationship/Title: _____ *Are they aware of this planner? (Y/N)*

Address: _____

Phone: _____ Email: _____

Notes: _____

LEGAL CONTACTS

Attorney

Attorney's Name: _____

Address: _____

Phone: _____ Email: _____

Notes: _____

Power of Attorney

Name: _____

Address: _____

Phone: _____ Email: _____

Notes: _____

Estate Executor

Name: _____

Address: _____

Phone: _____ Email: _____

Notes: _____

Tax Preparer

Name: _____

Address: _____

Phone: _____ Email: _____

Notes: _____

Trustee

Name: _____

Address: _____

Phone: _____ Email: _____

Notes: _____

Other

Name: _____

Address: _____

Phone: _____ Email: _____

Notes: _____

BUSINESS CONTACTS
Main Business Information

Business Name: _____

Legal Structure *(ex. LLC, S Corp, etc)*: _____

Business Type: _____

Business Address: _____

Phone: _____ Cell Phone Access Code: _____

Landlord's Name: _____

Contact Information: _____

Lease Documentation/Location of Keys Location: _____

Alarm Code Details and Instructions: _____

Business Website: _____

Username: _____ Password: _____

Primary Email: _____

Username: _____ Password: _____

Partner/Co-Owner Name: _____

Contact Information: _____

Partner/Co-Owner Name: _____

Contact Information: _____

Additional Instructions: _____

_____

Associates, Employees, and Contractors

Name/Company: _____

Contact Information: _____

Name/Company: _____

Contact Information: _____

Name/Company: _____

Contact Information: _____

Name/Company: _____

Contact Information: _____

Name/Company: _____

Contact Information: _____

Name/Company: _____

Contact Information: _____

Name/Company: _____

Contact Information: _____

Name/Company: _____

Contact Information: _____

Name/Company: _____

Contact Information: _____

Name/Company: _____

Contact Information: _____

"When we reach out, we extend a hand of hope, reminding others that they are not alone."   *- Unknown*

Play 2 Notes:

_____

_____

_____

_____

_____

_____

_____

_____

_____

_____

_____

_____

_____

_____

_____

_____

_____

_____

_____

_____

_____

_____

_____

Play 3: Medical

In this next play, we'll tackle recording your medical information. This will be invaluable for your designated emergency contact or caregiver, helping them answer any questions from medical personnel when the need arises.

- **HEALTH CARE INFORMATION**
  - Medical Power of Attorney
  - Healthcare Provider – Medical
  - Healthcare Provider – Dental
  - Healthcare Provider – Vision
  - Healthcare Provider – Other
  - Preferred Pharmacy
  - Caregiver(s)
  - Other
- **MEDICAL HISTORY**
  - Insurance
- **MEDICATIONS**
- **IN CASE OF INCAPACITATION**

TESTMONIAL

When my husband was diagnosed with cancer, it was a complete gut punch for me. At 36 years old, I wasn't expecting to have to plan for the possibility of my husband not being around. I, personally, had life insurance but that was the extent of my planning. Fran asked to meet with me to talk about planning. I was very reluctant to meet because I didn't want to be sad or cry about planning for my husband's end. However, I'm so glad I decided to follow through and meet with her. She gave me good insight and advice about what I should do to plan, not just for my husband, but for me too. She showed me that this was my opportunity to have control over my own affairs and set things the way I wanted them. She didn't make it feel like death was at my door either, which made having the conversation so much easier. I'm now more confident about what will happen if something were to happen to me or my husband because I have started setting my affairs in order. I plan for us to live for 60 more years, but in case we don't, my family won't have to stress about what to do!

- Kelley Perry

HEALTHCARE INFORMATION

Medical Power of Attorney

Full Name: _____

Address: _____

Phone: _____

Email: _____

Location of Documents: _____

Health Care Provider – Medical

Name/Practice: _____

Address: _____

Phone: _____ Website: _____

Email: _____

Notes: _____

Health Care Provider – Dental

Name/Practice: _____

Address: _____

Phone: _____ Website: _____

Email: _____

Notes: _____

Health Care Provider – Vision

Name/Practice: _____

Address: _____

Phone: _____ Website: _____

Email: _____

Notes: _____

Health Care Provider – Other

Name: _____

Address: _____

Phone: _____ Email: _____

Notes: _____

Preferred Pharmacy

Name: _____

Address: _____

Phone: _____ Website: _____

Email: _____

Notes: _____

Caregiver #1:

Name: _____

Address: _____

Phone: _____ Email: _____

Notes: _____

Caregiver #2:

Name: _____

Address: _____

Phone: _____ Email: _____

Notes: _____

Other

Name: _____

Address: _____

Phone: _____ Email: _____

Notes: _____

MEDICAL HISTORY

Blood Type: _____

Medical Conditions *(ex. Diabetic, Heart Condition, etc.)*: _____

_____

Allergies *(Include Drug Reactions)*: _____

_____

Vaccinations *(Include Dates)*: _____

_____

Family Medical History Summary: _____

_____

Medical Insurance

Primary Insurance Type: _____

Provider Name: _____

Phone: _____

Website: _____

Username: _____ Password: _____

Member Number: _____

Group Number: _____

Primary Member: _____

Location of Documents: _____

Secondary Insurance Type: _____

Provider Name: _____

Phone: _____

Website: _____

Username: _____ Password: _____

Member Number: _____

Group Number: _____

Primary Member: _____

Location of Documents: _____

Secondary Insurance Type: _____

Provider Name: _____

Phone: _____

Website: _____

Username: _____ Password: _____

Member Number: _____

Group Number: _____

Primary Member: _____

Location of Documents: _____

Other Insurance Type: _____

Provider Name: _____

Phone: _____

Website: _____

Username: _____ Password: _____

Member Number: _____

Group Number: _____

Primary Member: _____

Location of Documents: _____

MEDICATIONS

Medication #1: _____

Taken for: _____ Dosage: _____ Frequency: _____

Pharmacy: _____ Phone: _____

Additional Info: _____

Medication #2: _____

Taken for: _____ Dosage: _____ Frequency: _____

Pharmacy: _____ Phone: _____

Additional Info: _____

Medication #3: _____

Taken for: _____ Dosage: _____ Frequency: _____

Pharmacy: _____ Phone: _____

Additional Info: _____

Medication #4: _____

Taken for: _____ Dosage: _____ Frequency: _____

Pharmacy: _____ Phone: _____

Additional Info: _____

Medication #5: _____

Taken for: _____ Dosage: _____ Frequency: _____

Pharmacy: _____ Phone: _____

Additional Info: _____

Medication #6: _____

Taken for: _____ Dosage: _____ Frequency: _____

Pharmacy: _____ Phone: _____

Additional Info: _____

Medication #7: _____

Taken for: _____ Dosage: _____ Frequency: _____

Pharmacy: _____ Phone: _____

Additional Info: _____

Medication #8: _____

Taken for: _____ Dosage: _____ Frequency: _____

Pharmacy: _____ Phone: _____

Additional Info: _____

IN CASE OF INCAPACITATION

Preference(s) if unable to care for myself:

- Stay at home with _____

- Stay at home with a hired caregiver

  Cost: $_____

- Move in with _____

- Stay at a care facility: _____

  Cost: $_____

Website: _____

Address: _____

Phone: _____

Contact person: _____

Care will be paid by: _____

Details for how care will be paid: _____

_____

Preferred Caregiver Name: _____

Do you have Do Not Resuscitate (DNR) legal documentation?

- If yes, where are they located?

  _____

- If not, provide your DNR Instructions here and get legal documentation completed:

  _____

  _____

Organ donor instructions and formal document location:

_____

Additional information & preferences if incapacitated:

_____

_____

_____

_____

_____

"Be thankful for today, because in one moment, your entire life could change."
— Unknown

Play 3 Notes:

_____

_____

_____

_____

_____

_____

_____

_____

_____

_____

_____

_____

_____

_____

_____

_____

_____

_____

_____

_____

_____

_____

_____

Play 4: Finances

In this next play, we're diving into your finances. It's all about jotting down important financial information so your emergency contact can step in if needed. Make sure to lay out simple instructions on how bills and such should be taken care of.

- **BILLS**
- **DEBTS**
- **CREDIT AND DEBIT CARDS**
- **BANK ACCOUNTS**
- **INVESTMENTS**
- **RETIREMENT**
- **SAFES AND SAFE DEPOSIT BOXES**
- **HIDDEN CASH**
- **FINANCE APPS**
- **ADDITIONAL ASSETS**

TESTMONIAL

Francina Raynor has been helping families and friends for years. We are so blessed that she has taken her knowledge and experience in the areas of pre-planning and estate securing to share to empower us. She has provided this guide with intentional strategies to secure legacy and stability for families. Francina will create a paradigm shift in the way that we prepare and plan for our transition, and that of loved ones, from this life to eternity. This workbook promises to be one of the best resources for families to have in their possession. It will elevate the mindset and culture of this generation and others for years to come.

"Who is wise and understanding among you? Let them show it by their good life, by deeds done in the humility that comes from wisdom." **– James 3:13**

- Tanya Young

BILLS

Company Name: _____

Account Type *(ex. utilities)*: _____

Account Number: _____

Auto Debit (Y/N) Due Date *(ex. 3rd)*: _____ Phone: _____

Website: _____

Username: _____ Password: _____

Company Name: _____

Account Type *(ex. utilities)*: _____

Account Number: _____

Auto Debit (Y/N) Due Date *(ex. 3rd)*: _____ Phone: _____

Website: _____

Username: _____ Password: _____

Company Name: _____

Account Type *(ex. utilities)*: _____

Account Number: _____

Auto Debit (Y/N) Due Date *(ex. 3rd)*: _____ Phone: _____

Website: _____

Username: _____ Password: _____

Company Name: _____

Account Type *(ex. utilities)*: _____

Account Number: _____

Auto Debit (Y/N) Due Date *(ex. 3rd)*: _____ Phone: _____

Website: _____

Username: _____ Password: _____

DEBTS

Company Name: _____

Account Type *(ex. Auto, Mortgage, Student Loans, Credit Cards)*: _____

Account Number: _____

Phone: _____

Website: _____

Username: _____ Password: _____

Balance: _____ Remaining Term: _____

Payment: _____ Auto Debit: (Y/N)   Due Date *(ex. 3rd)*: _____

Company Name: _____

Account Type *(ex. Auto, Mortgage, Student Loans, Credit Cards)*: _____

Account Number: _____

Phone: _____

Website: _____

Username: _____ Password: _____

Balance: _____ Remaining Term: _____

Payment: _____ Auto Debit: (Y/N)   Due Date *(ex. 3rd)*: _____

Company Name: _____

Account Type *(ex. Auto, Mortgage, Student Loans, Credit Cards)*: _____

Account Number: _____

Phone: _____

Website: _____

Username: _____ Password: _____

Balance: _____ Remaining Term: _____

Payment: _____ Auto Debit: (Y/N)   Due Date *(ex. 3rd)*: _____

CREDIT AND DEBIT CARDS

Type *(ex. Credit, Bank, Gas)*: _____

Company Name: _____

Name(s) On Card: _____

Card Number: _____

Exp. Date: _____ CVV Code: _____ PIN: _____

Phone: _____ Website: _____

Username: _____ Password: _____

Notes: _____

_____

Type *(ex. Credit, Bank, Gas)*: _____

Company Name: _____

Name(s) On Card: _____

Card Number: _____

Exp. Date: _____ CVV Code: _____ PIN: _____

Phone: _____ Website: _____

Username: _____ Password: _____

Notes: _____

_____

Type *(ex. Credit, Bank, Gas)*: _____

Company Name: _____

Name(s) On Card: _____

Card Number: _____

Exp. Date: _____ CVV Code: _____ PIN: _____

Phone: _____ Website: _____

Username: _____ Password: _____

Notes: _____

_____

Type *(ex. Credit, Bank, Gas)*: _____

Company Name: _____

Name(s) On Card: _____

Card Number: _____

Exp. Date: _____ CVV Code: _____ PIN: _____

Phone: _____ Website: _____

Username: _____ Password: _____

Notes: _____

_____

Type *(ex. Credit, Bank, Gas)*: _____

Company Name: _____

Name(s) On Card: _____

Card Number: _____

Exp. Date: _____ CVV Code: _____ PIN: _____

Phone: _____ Website: _____

Username: _____ Password: _____

Notes: _____

_____

Type *(ex. Credit, Bank, Gas)*: _____

Company Name: _____

Name(s) On Card: _____

Card Number: _____

Exp. Date: _____ CVV Code: _____ PIN: _____

Phone: _____ Website: _____

Username: _____ Password: _____

Notes: _____

_____

BANK ACCOUNTS

Checking, Savings, CDs, etc.

Please ensure that all the listed accounts have designated beneficiaries. Assigning beneficiaries to these accounts might negate the necessity for a will for the funds to be accessed. However, it's important to note that they will still require a death certificate.

Account Type *(ex. Checking, Savings)*: _____

Bank Name: _____

Account Number: _____

Name(s) on Account: _____

Address: _____

Phone: _____

Beneficiaries: _____

Location of Documents: _____

Online information

    Website: _____

    Login / Username: _____ Password: _____

Notes *(ex. Pin Number)*: _____

Account Type *(ex. Checking, Savings)*: _____

Bank Name: _____

Account Number: _____

Name(s) on Account: _____

Address: _____

Phone: _____

Beneficiaries: _____

Location of Documents: _____

Online information

    Website: _____

    Login / Username: _____ Password: _____

Notes *(ex. Pin Number)*: _____

Account Type *(ex. Checking, Savings)*: _____

Bank Name: _____

Account Number: _____

Name(s) on Account: _____

Address: _____

Phone: _____

Beneficiaries: _____

Location of Documents: _____

Online information

    Website: _____

    Login / Username: _____ Password: _____

Notes *(ex. Pin Number)*: _____

Account Type *(ex. Checking, Savings)*: _____

Bank Name: _____

Account Number: _____

Name(s) on Account: _____

Address: _____

Phone: _____

Beneficiaries: _____

Location of Documents: _____

Online information

    Website: _____

    Login / Username: _____ Password: _____

Notes *(ex. Pin Number)*: _____

INVESTMENTS

Investment Type *(ex. Stock, Bond, Fund, Annuity)*: _____

Financial Institution: _____

Account Number: _____

Name(s) on Account: _____

Address: _____

Phone: _____

Beneficiaries: _____

Location of Documents: _____

Online information

    Website: _____

    Username: _____ Password: _____

Notes: _____

Investment Type *(ex. Stock, Bond, Fund, Annuity)*: _____

Financial Institution: _____

Account Number: _____

Name(s) on Account: _____

Address: _____

Phone: _____

Beneficiaries: _____

Location of Documents: _____

Online information

    Website: _____

    Username: _____ Password: _____

Notes: _____

Investment Type *(ex. Stock, Bond, Fund, Annuity)*: _____

Financial Institution: _____

Account Number: _____

Name(s) on Account: _____

Address: _____

Phone: _____

Beneficiaries: _____

Location of Documents: _____

Online information

    Website: _____

    Username: _____ Password: _____

Notes: _____

Investment Type *(ex. Stock, Bond, Fund, Annuity)*: _____

Financial Institution: _____

Account Number: _____

Name(s) on Account: _____

Address: _____

Phone: _____

Beneficiaries: _____

Location of Documents: _____

Online information

    Website: _____

    Username: _____ Password: _____

Notes: _____

RETIREMENT

Retirement Type *(ex. Pension, SSI, 401k, IRA)*: _____

Provider/Employer/Government: _____

Name(s) on Account: _____

Address: _____

Phone: _____

Beneficiaries: _____

Online information

Website: _____ Username: _____ Password: _____

Notes *(include location)*: _____

Retirement Type *(ex. Pension, SSI, 401k, IRA)*: _____

Provider/Employer/Government: _____

Name(s) on Account: _____

Address: _____

Phone: _____

Beneficiaries: _____

Online information

Website: _____ Username: _____ Password: _____

Notes *(include location)*: _____

Retirement Type *(ex. Pension, SSI, 401k, IRA)*: _____

Provider/Employer/Government: _____

Name(s) on Account: _____

Address: _____

Phone: _____

Beneficiaries: _____

Online information

Website: _____ Username: _____ Password: _____

Notes *(include location)*: _____

SAFES AND SAFE DEPOSIT BOXES

If you opt for the safety deposit box, ensure there is a trusted individual who is authorized to access it as a signer at the bank.

Safe Description: _____

Location: _____

Access Details: _____

Safe Deposit Box Bank Name *(if needed)*: _____

Address: _____

Phone: _____

Box Number: _____

Contact Info for Authorized Persons: _____

Summary of Safe Contents: _____

_____

_____

Safe Description: _____

Location: _____

Access Details: _____

Safe Deposit Box Bank Name *(if needed)*: _____

Address: _____

Phone: _____

Box Number: _____

Contact Info for Authorized Persons: _____

Summary of Safe Contents: _____

_____

_____

HIDDEN CASH

Estimated Value: _____

Purpose of Cash: _____

Location: _____

Access Details: _____

Person With Knowledge of Cash: _____

- • Phone: _____

- • Address: _____

- • Email: _____

Notes: _____

Estimated Value: _____

Purpose of Cash: _____

Location: _____

Access Details: _____

Person With Knowledge of Cash: _____

- • Phone: _____

- • Address: _____

- • Email: _____

Notes: _____

Details On Other Hidden Valuables: _____

_____

_____

_____

_____

_____

_____

_____

_____

FINANCE APPS

App *(ex. Cash App, Zelle, Venmo)*: _____

Name on account: _____

Account ID or number: _____

Username: _____ Password: _____

Card Number: _____ PIN: _____

Notes: _____

App *(ex. Cash App, Zelle, Venmo)*: _____

Name on account: _____

Account ID or number: _____

Username: _____ Password: _____

Card Number: _____ PIN: _____

Notes: _____

App *(ex. Cash App, Zelle, Venmo)*: _____

Name on account: _____

Account ID or number: _____

Username: _____ Password: _____

Card Number: _____ PIN: _____

Notes: _____

App *(ex. Cash App, Zelle, Venmo)*: _____

Name on account: _____

Account ID or number: _____

Username: _____ Password: _____

Card Number: _____ PIN: _____

Notes: _____

ADDITIONAL ASSETS

Item #1: _____

Company: _____

Phone: _____

Account Number: _____

Website: _____

Co-Owners And / Or Beneficiaries on Account: _____

Location of Documents: _____

Item #2: _____

Company: _____

Phone: _____

Account Number: _____

Website: _____

Co-Owners And / Or Beneficiaries on Account: _____

Location of Documents: _____

Item #3: _____

Company: _____

Phone: _____

Account Number: _____

Website: _____

Co-Owners And / Or Beneficiaries on Account: _____

Location of Documents: _____

Item #4: _____

Company: _____

Phone: _____

Account Number: _____

Website: _____

Co-Owners And / Or Beneficiaries on Account: _____

Location of Documents: _____

"It always seems impossible until it is done."   *– Nelson Mandela*

Play 4 Notes:

_____

_____

_____

_____

_____

_____

_____

_____

_____

_____

_____

_____

_____

_____

_____

_____

_____

_____

_____

_____

_____

_____

_____

_____

_____

_____

Play 5: Security

In this play, you'll record important information like passwords, alarm codes, where you stash keys, and other details your emergency contact might need.

- **PASSWORDS**
- **SECURITY QUESTIONS**
- **CODES**
  - Alarms
  - Phones
  - Computers
- **LOCATION OF IMPORTANT DOCUMENTS**
- **DESCRIPTION AND LOCATION OF KEYS**

TESTMONIAL

"If you ever need anyone to help you in your time of need, Fran Raynor is the person for you. I can't say enough about Fran. She will always get the job done! You will never have to worry about delays because Fran will have it done yesterday! All things concerning my family's business were impeccably done, with no delays! If you want it done right the first time, please contact Fran. My family and I are forever grateful for her services and consulting."

- Brian Sullivan

PASSWORDS

Email, social media apps (ex. Facebook, LinkedIn, etc.)

App: _____

Email: _____

Username: _____ Password: _____

Notes: _____

App: _____

Email: _____

Username: _____ Password: _____

Notes: _____

App: _____

Email: _____

Username: _____ Password: _____

Notes: _____

App: _____

Email: _____

Username: _____ Password: _____

Notes: _____

App: _____

Email: _____

Username: _____ Password: _____

Notes: _____

App: _____

Email: _____

Username: _____ Password: _____

Notes: _____

SECURITY QUESTIONS

Examples of security questions include:
Mother's maiden name, your favorite teacher, the make and model of your first car, etc.

Question: _____

Answer: _____

Question: _____

Answer: _____

Question: _____

Answer: _____

Question: _____

Answer: _____

Question: _____

Answer: _____

Question: _____

Answer: _____

Question: _____

Answer: _____

Question: _____

Answer: _____

Question: _____

Answer: _____

Question: _____

Answer: _____

CODES
Alarm

Alarm Location: _____ Access Code: _____

Monitoring Company: _____

Phone: _____

Notes (ex. Verbal Password): _____

Cell Phone

Cell Phone Number: _____

Cell Phone Code: _____ Voicemail Pin: _____

Description of Phone: _____

Service Carrier: _____

Phone: _____

Website: _____

Username: _____ Password: _____

Notes: _____

Computer

Computer/Tablet/Device: _____

Description *(ex. brand, color)*: _____

Access Method/Code: _____

Other Access Details: _____

Computer/Tablet/Device: _____

Description *(ex. brand, color)*: _____

Access Method/Code: _____

Other Access Details: _____

Computer/Tablet/Device: _____

Description *(ex. brand, color)*: _____

Access Method/Code: _____

Other Access Details: _____

LOCATION OF IMPORTANT DOCUMENTS

List the location (safe, address, etc.) where someone could find the following documents in case of an emergency. If electronic documents are online, provide the website or application name and login credentials.

Personal

Adoption Papers: _____

Birth Certificate: _____

Custody Papers: _____

Divorce Papers: _____

DD 214 (military): _____

Driver's License: _____

Social Security Card: _____

Marriage Certificate: _____

Passport: _____

Tax Documents: _____

Notes: _____

Health Insurance

Life Insurance: _____

Health insurance - Medical: _____

Health Insurance - Dental: _____

Health insurance - Vision: _____

Health Insurance - Other: _____

Health Insurance - Other: _____

Funeral Insurance: _____

Insurance

Vehicle Insurance #1: _____

Vehicle Insurance #2: _____

Homeowner Insurance: _____

Rental Home Insurance: _____

Life Insurance: _____

Insurance for Child #1: _____

Insurance for Child #2: _____

Insurance for Child #3: _____

Other Family / Dependents Insurance: _____

Notes: _____

Estate plan

Will: _____

Power of attorney

Health Care Power of Attorney Documents: _____

Dual Power of Attorney Documents: _____

Other

Document Type: _____

Location: _____

Document Type: _____

Location: _____

Document Type: _____

Location: _____

Document Type: _____

Location: _____

Document Type: _____

Location: _____

Document Type: _____

Location: _____

DESCRIPTION AND LOCATION OF KEYS

Physical Description of Key: _____

This Key Unlocks: _____

Location of Key: _____

Notes *(ex. Does anyone have a copy?)*: _____

Physical Description of Key: _____

This Key Unlocks: _____

Location of Key: _____

Notes *(ex. Does anyone have a copy?)*: _____

Physical Description of Key: _____

This Key Unlocks: _____

Location of Key: _____

Notes *(ex. Does anyone have a copy?)*: _____

Physical Description of Key: _____

This Key Unlocks: _____

Location of Key: _____

Notes *(ex. Does anyone have a copy?)*: _____

Physical Description of Key: _____

This Key Unlocks: _____

Location of Key: _____

Notes *(ex. Does anyone have a copy?)*: _____

Physical Description of Key: _____

This Key Unlocks: _____

Location of Key: _____

Notes *(ex. Does anyone have a copy?)*: _____

"Sometimes in life, a sudden situation occurs, a moment in time, alters your whole life, forever changes the road ahead." — *Ahmad Ardalan*

Play 5 Notes:

Play 6: The Final Play

In this last play, you will record details of your final wishes to your loved ones to ensure your affairs are taken care of the way you want them.

- **FINAL AFFAIRS**
  - Funeral Arrangements
  - Funeral Details
  - Burial Details
- **FINAL EXPENSES**

TESTMONIAL

Ms. Fran Raynor coordinated homegoing services for my husband. Ms. Raynor led the preparation of services for my husband in a seamless manner. I provided Ms. Raynor with the information needed, and she handled every little detail of the service. She organized the program, and it represented my husband well from the theme to the order of service. Her services were needed during the pandemic, and she ensured the safety of all who attended. The services went on without any problems. All my family and I had to do was show up on that day to celebrate the life of my husband. I feel confident in referring Fran to my family and friends.

- Rachiel P. Durant

FINAL AFFAIRS

The person I prefer to handle my final wishes:

Name: _____

Address: _____

Phone: _____ Email: _____

Notes: _____

I prefer to have a:

_____ - Traditional Burial _____ - Cremation _____ - Interment at Burial Site

_____ - Other: _____

_____ - Or let the following person decide:

  • Name: _____

  • Address: _____

  • Phone: _____ Email: _____

If I am cremated, I would like my ashes:

  • Placed in an urn & given to: _____

  • Scattered (where): _____

  • Other: _____

Instructions, Preferences, Invite List, and Other Documents for Final Arrangements are located here: _____

Funeral Arrangements

Answer the following questions regarding what type of funeral service you would like to have:

1. I want to have a religious service.
   No / Yes

2. I want to have a military service.
   No / Yes

3. I want to have a viewing. No / Yes

4. I want to have a wake. No / Yes

5. I want to have an open casket.
   No / Yes

6. I want to have a closed casket.
   No / Yes

7. I want to have a graveside ceremony.
   No / Yes

Notes: _____

_____

_____

Funeral Insurance Policy: _____

    • Company Name: _____

    • Contact Information: _____

Funeral Home: _____

    • Address: _____

    • Contact Information: _____

Funeral Location: _____

    • Contact Information: _____

Other Funeral Details

Casket selection: _____

Flower selection(s): _____

Obituary Information: _____

_____

_____

_____

Other Requests *(ex. Pallbearers, Eulogy Speaker, Music, Flowers)*: _____

_____

_____

_____

_____

_____

_____

Burial Details

Headstone description: _____

Company: _____

Plot Information: _____

Cemetery or Crematorium: _____

    • Address: _____

    • Contact Information: _____

FINAL EXPENSES

Expenses to be paid *(ex. Life Insurance, Prepaid Memorial, etc.)*:

Company: _____

Policy/Account Number: _____

Address: _____

Contact Person: _____

Phone: _____

Location of Documents: _____

Online information:

    Website: _____

    Username: _____ Password: _____

Company: _____

Policy/Account Number: _____

Address: _____

Contact Person: _____

Phone: _____

Location of Documents: _____

Online information:

    Website: _____

    Username: _____ Password: _____

Company: _____

Policy/Account Number: _____

Address: _____

Contact Person: _____

Phone: _____

Location of Documents: _____

Online information:

    Website: _____

    Username: _____ Password: _____

Company: _____

Policy/Account Number: _____

Address: _____

Contact Person: _____

Phone: _____

Location of Documents: _____

Online information:

    Website: _____

    Username: _____ Password: _____

Company: _____

Policy/Account Number: _____

Address: _____

Contact Person: _____

Phone: _____

Location of Documents: _____

Online information:

    Website: _____

    Username: _____ Password: _____

Other things to consider

Here is where you can list bills or services that need to be canceled, paid, or placed in someone else's name (such as phone, internet, cards, autopay, banking, etc.)

Company: _____

Contact Information: _____

Account Number: _____

Username and Password: _____

Notes: _____

Company: _____

Contact Information: _____

Account Number: _____

Username and Password: _____

Notes: _____

Company: _____

Contact Information: _____

Account Number: _____

Username and Password: _____

Notes: _____

Company: _____

Contact Information: _____

Account Number: _____

Username and Password: _____

Notes: _____

Company: _____

Contact Information: _____

Account Number: _____

Username and Password: _____

Notes: _____

Company: _____

Contact Information: _____

Account Number: _____

Username and Password: _____

Notes: _____

"I don't just talk about change. I actually have a plan to execute change and make it happen."   *— Unknown*

Play 6 Notes:

_____

_____

_____

_____

_____

_____

_____

_____

_____

_____

_____

_____

_____

_____

_____

_____

_____

_____

_____

_____

_____

_____

_____

_____

_____

KEY TERMS

TOD: Transfer On Death deed if you own a home. Completing this document and filing it with your county saves your heirs thousands of dollars. This document allows you to transfer ownership of your home to your designee. All they need to do is take their ID and your death certificate to the county building and the deed is signed over. Doing this will avoid the home having to go through probate.

Living Will: Allows you to put in writing exactly what you want done in the event you cannot speak for yourself when it comes to healthcare decisions as well as other final decisions.

Durable Power of Attorney: Allows you to designate a person to make legal decisions if you are no longer competent to do so.

Power of Attorney for Healthcare: This document allows you to designate someone to make healthcare decisions for you.

Last Will and Testament: Designates to whom personal belongings will go and who the Administrator will be. But if you have a beneficiary on any of your financial accounts, that will override a will. For instance, if you say, "I leave all of my possessions to my son Adam", but on your savings account the beneficiary is your best friend, then the money goes to your best friend.

Funeral Planning Declaration: Allows you to say exactly what your wishes are as far as the disposition of the body and the services.

NOTE: A last will and testament creates instructions for your executor regarding the disposition of your assets. You may want to avoid probate. A common way to do so is to put all your assets in a trust or to make sure all your assets have a joint owner or beneficiary. This playbook is not intended to be legal advice and we recommend seeking assistance from a lawyer regarding setting up your estate or a trust.

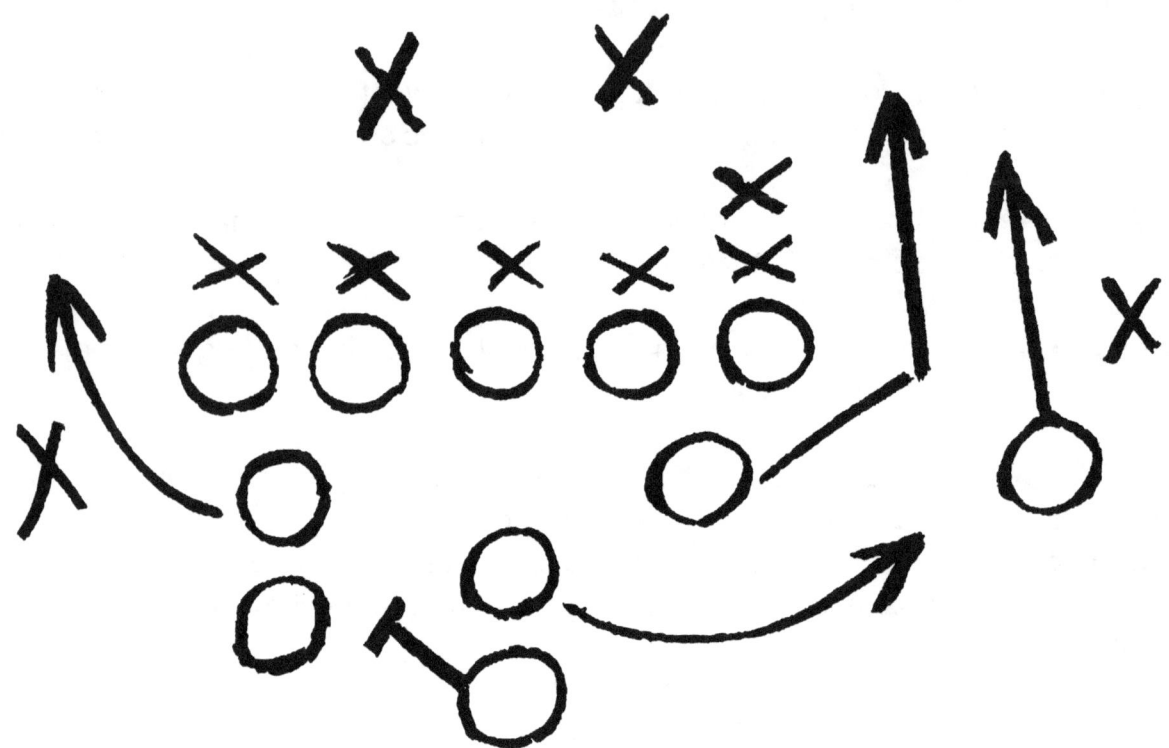

The legacy continues...

www.ingramcontent.com/pod-product-compliance
Lightning Source LLC
Chambersburg PA
CBHW081008120626
46546CB00010B/3069